88 Secrets to Success for Your Short-Term Rental Business

John & Wynde Williams

Table Of Contents

DEDICATION

This book is dedicated to our mentors and teachers along the way. We wouldn't be where we are without their guidance and support.

INTRODUCTION

This book is organized a little differently than what many readers may be used to. It is not meant to be a complete "how-to" on everything short-term rental, but it will show you how to handle key areas in your business. It is not meant to be read like a chapter book from beginning to end, although you can. We wrote this book with the intention that the reader could turn to any section and find useful information to use in his or her own business. These are some of the most valuable "secrets" we have learned along the way. We hope that you find them valuable as well.

SECTION ONE: FOUNDATIONAL KNOWLEDGE

#1: DECIDE ON A TARGET CUSTOMER FIRST

Before you find a property, before you start the design, before you do anything, think about whom you wish to serve. Answering this one question first will guide you in every other decision you will make. There are so many different types of customers out there from business travelers to traveling nurses to families. Choose one based on your area or one that you can relate to. We serve families with children coming into town for life events such as weddings, funerals and family reunions because that is who we are, and we can relate to them. We can anticipate what they will need before they even arrive.

Choosing a target customer first will help you decide where your property should be. If you are catering to business travelers, you will most likely need to find a property in a city or one near public transportation. If you are going to serve traveling nurses, it would make sense to choose a location close to a hospital. When we look for locations, we look for a nice, quiet, safe residential neighborhood because that's where our guests want to be.

Your target customer will also dictate what type of property you should be looking for. Business travelers are more likely to travel alone and don't need as much room as a whole family. Therefore, a smaller unit would suit them fine whereas a family will need a much larger space such as a whole house. Families are more likely to want more privacy as well so they would be more comfortable in a single-family home than a cramped condo or apartment.

What you put into your unit will also be determined by whom you are serving. A business traveler will appreciate a printer, but a family won't have any use for it. A family with small children will appreciate a highchair and a pack n' play but an older couple won't have any use for it. Once you've determined who your target customer will be, it will be your guiding principle in everything else that you do.

One mistake that people make as they are starting their short-term rental business is that they find a property first and then try to determine who might want to stay there. From our point of view, this is working backwards. The problem with this approach is that, as you add units, they inevitably will be suited to different customer types. This means that, instead of focusing your marketing, customer service, and other resources on a specific customer type, you are stuck trying to be all things to all people. This puts you at a disadvantage compared to someone else who has taken the time to define who they are and who they serve.

#2: LOCATION! LOCATION! LOCATION!

Just like in the real estate business, location is important in the short-term rental business as well. For example, in residential real estate, we often think of location in terms of where people want to live. We think of things like school districts, proximity to work centers, and availability of public transportation. While some of these factors may be important to where a short-term rental is located, others don't matter as much.

When you are trying to determine the best location for a new unit, the first thing you should do is to answer the question, "What customers are you serving?". Think about whom you want to serve and why they are coming to the area. Are they coming to visit family? Perhaps they would be more comfortable in a single-family home in a nice, safe neighborhood close to their family members. Are they business travelers coming on business? They may need to be close to public transportation and business centers. An apartment or condo might be a better fit. Are you serving traveling medical professionals? A location near a major hospital may be ideal.

Putting some thought into who your target customer is will tell you most of what you need to know about where to locate your units.

#3: READ THE HOA RULES

You must play by the rules, especially if you plan on being in business for any length of time. This means verifying that short term rentals are allowed in the area in which your unit is located. Cities and HOAs are really starting to crack down on short term rental operators that are operating unlawfully. Your reputation is everything in this business and you don't want to get a reputation for not acting ethically.

If your unit has an HOA, verify that the rules allow rentals less than 30 days because some do not, especially in newer neighborhoods. One of the first things you need to do is read up on the Covenants,

Conditions & Restrictions (CC&Rs) to verify short term rentals are allowed in the area.

Another thing that you might consider is to just avoid neighborhoods or buildings with an HOA in the first place. Just because they currently allow short-term rentals doesn't mean that the rules can't be changed.

SECTION TWO: WHAT TO PUT IN YOUR UNIT

#4: PROVIDE A COMMUNITY GUIDE

Out-of-town guests may be coming for any number of reasons; business, weddings, family reunions, sporting events, etc. When we first started, we knew we wanted to put something in the units that gave guests an idea about the area, sort of like a community guide. We searched on the local Chamber of Commerce website to see what they had to offer. There, we found a guide available on sporting events, new restaurants, shopping, arts and culture, breweries, and transportation. If you can't find a ready-made guide, consider making your own. A guide like this enriches a guest's experience, giving them a better understanding of the area. It can be a useful tool as they explore all that your city has to offer. If you expect to host international travelers, don't forget to include insights into local customs, meal times, bank holidays, traditions, ways of greeting and how to tip.

#5: CREATE A HOUSE MANUAL

Your house manual tells guests everything they need to know about staying in the unit. We purchase 3-ring leather binders and brand them with our company logo. The House Manual is divided into eleven sections with tabs for each section (another reason to use the label maker!). In the first section, we have a welcome page that says thank you for staying with us here at Queen City Suites. At the bottom, we tell people how they can book directly through our website. We include information about the Wi-Fi network and password. The next page is where we tell guests to contact us through the messaging platform and about how the review system works. The second section is about parking; where to park, where not to park, if there's a garage door code, etc. The third section is about how to work the security system. In the fourth section, we familiarize the guests with the amenities of the unit. For example, we describe what items are available in the kitchen and where to find them, how to operate the washer and dryer, how to use the TVs and how to work the thermostat. The fifth section is where we list the house rules. The sixth section is about emergencies. We tell guests to dial 911, but we also talk about how to handle maintenance emergencies and the closest urgent care facility. The seventh section is about our favorite restaurants and bars. The eighth section is about local attractions including addresses and phone numbers and websites. The ninth section is about the airport. The tenth section is about the closest grocery stores with addresses. And finally, the last section provides detailed checkout instructions.

On the inside pockets, we leave business cards that guests can take with them so that they know how to contact us for future stays. And there you have it; a beautifully organized, no-frills, easy-to-read Guest Book that guests will actually use and appreciate.

#6: DUVET COVERS ARE YOUR FRIEND!

The bed is the most important piece of furniture in the bedroom. It's the centerpiece. The first thing you see when you walk in a bedroom is the bed. A beautiful bed is key to a stunning bedroom. If the bed is messy and not put together well, all the other beautiful furniture in the room will not matter. The bed is king.

When it comes to creating a gorgeous bed, you basically have two choices; a comforter or a duvet cover. We choose to use duvet covers. A duvet cover is basically just a pillowcase for your comforter. It's a protective layer that slips over the comforter and has either a zipper closure or a button closure. We prefer the button closures because the zippers tend to break so often, which means we have to purchase another cover. Buttons are easy to sew on and don't seem to come off as often. The button closure duvet covers do take a little longer to put on, however.

Because comforters are difficult and expensive to clean, duvet covers are useful because they not only protect the comforter, it's also more sanitary. They are easy to remove and a lot less expensive to clean.

We purchase oversized king comforters and oversized king duvet covers for all of our beds, king and queen alike. We like the oversized ones because they hang a little lower, giving the bed a lush, expensive look. We used to buy just plain duvet covers but they show wrinkles and look messy. Now we get the pleated ones which hide wrinkles. They look really great in pictures, too!

#7: BUY ALL FLAT SHEETS

Buying all flat sheets instead of flat and fitted can make it so much easier for your cleaners! Professional laundry services have an uncanny ability to fold a fitted sheet so that you can't tell the difference between fitted sheets and flat sheets when they're folded so neatly (how do they do that??). Instead of your cleaners wasting time trying to figure out if a sheet is a fitted sheet or a flat sheet, just buy all flat sheets.

Flat sheets can also be fitted sheets. A flat sheet can be tucked in on all sides to resemble a fitted sheet. King size flat sheets can fit just as well on queen size beds as both fitted sheets and flat sheets. So, buy all King size flat sheets no matter what size beds you have.

Not only will this save you time, but it will save you money. You can buy sets of King flat sheets in bulk quantities. Just remember that you need 2 per bed per turnover. We like to purchase enough linens for 4 turnovers. For example, for 1 bed, you will need to purchase 8 flat sheets (4 x 2 = 8). Likewise, if you have 2 beds, you will need to purchase 16 flat sheets.

#8: IF YOU HAVE DIFFERENT SIZE BEDS, BUY ALL OF YOUR SHEETS IN THE SAME SIZE AS THE LARGEST ONE

Most of our units have a king size bed in the master bedroom and a queen size bed in all the other bedrooms. The sleeper sofas are also queen size. Instead of buying king and queen size sheets, we buy all king size sheets. King size sheets can fit just as well on queen size beds. Buying all king size sheets saves us time and money.

It will save you money by buying in bulk. We buy ours on Amazon. And it saves time since the cleaners won't have to figure out if that sheet is the correct size for the bed they are making up. They can just grab 2 sheets and go.

#9: PUT A MATTRESS PROTECTOR ON EVERY BED

Even if you are not serving families with children like we do, you should still put a mattress protector on every bed because, well, people are leaky. If you've ever had to clean up after anyone, children, adults, pets, you know what we're talking about. It is what it is. So be prepared.

Have an extra on hand for accidents. Keep it in the bedroom closet in a clear container and label it. Make sure your cleaners know about it. Mattress protectors can be washed.

It's best to buy the zippered mattress encasement that goes around the entire mattress. These are not only waterproof, but they also guard against dust mites, allergens, bacteria, mold and mildew. Most importantly, they guard against bed bugs.

#10: PROVIDE A METAL LUGGAGE RACK IN EACH BEDROOM

If you don't provide a dresser, which we typically don't, a great alternative is to provide a luggage rack. Guests who are staying for a short time will live out of their suitcases and will appreciate not having to bend over because their suitcase is on the floor. It's a nice touch and makes your guests feel considered.

But don't use a wooden one! Instead, opt for metal. This helps to prevent bed bugs. Bed bugs can easily climb wooden surfaces. This is a great tip when traveling as well. Never put your suitcase on a wooden luggage rack.

#11: PROVIDE A FULL-LENGTH MIRROR

Guests love having a full-length mirror in their room when they are visiting. Because we cater to families coming to town for weddings, funerals and family reunions, most of our guests are going to be dressing up during their stay with us. Therefore, providing a full-length mirror allows guests to make sure their attire is perfect.

Mirrors can also be used as decoration. They don't get enough attention in most designs, in our opinion. Mirrors can really help transform a room! They can be mounted on walls or be free-standing. They can be framed or not. Mirrors are extremely versatile in that they can represent any decor style from modern to minimalist. Adding a mirror to a room instantly transforms any small room from cozy to roomy. Design and function!

#12: USE ALL WHITE TOWELS AND SHEETS

Colors may look great for design purposes but to scale and keep things more sanitary, you're going to want a professional laundry service to bleach everything. So just buy all white everything. The hotels do it for a reason and so should you! If you're feeling drab and dull with all white, throw a decorative throw blanket and some accent pillows on the bed. You'll be feeling bright and cheery in no time.

#13: HAVE AT LEAST FOUR SETS OF TOWELS FOR EACH BATHROOM

We define a set as the number typically left out for your guests to use during their stay. For example, if your unit has one bathroom and can sleep four people, a set would be four, at a minimum.

One set will be clean in the unit for the current guest, the second set will be dirty from the previous guest and sent to the laundry, the third set is for backup and replacement purposes, and the fourth set is for "oops" and holidays. Occasionally, on certain holidays like Labor Day in the United States, the laundry may not be open and running. That's when you will need that fourth set.

Make sure you purchase enough towels when you are setting up your unit. In the above example, with one bathroom that requires four towels, you will need to purchase 16 towels (4 x 4 = 16). There's nothing worse than a late-night run to the store or having to place a last-minute order on Amazon, praying for same-day shipping. Because accidents will happen, be prepared. Your guests will thank you for having the forethought to avoid this issue.

#14: PROVIDE PERSONAL BATHROOM AMENITIES

Guests are not just looking for a bed to sleep in or a roof over their heads anymore. They have become quite savvy and demanding. They want to feel welcomed, even pampered, dare we say lavished. If you want to stand out, you need to exceed guest expectations on the basics. Bathroom amenities such as a hair dryer, cotton balls, cotton swabs, shampoo, conditioner, body wash, bar soap and makeup wipes are basic amenities that guests will expect to see when they stay at your unit.

The refillable containers you find at some hotels mounted on the wall in the shower are all fine and dandy. But they get leaky after a while which means more cleaning for your cleaning crew. And sometimes people will be mean and put something other than what's intended in there believe it or not.

Your best bet is to leave out good quality amenities. Leave them neatly arranged in the bathroom on the vanity where guests will see them. After a long car ride or plane ride, guests want nothing more than to take a shower and go to bed. Save them the hassle of having to dig around in their luggage for soap and shampoo. They probably forgot to pack it anyway.

Pro tip: Be sure to have the photographer take pictures of the amenities as well. Remember, if it's not in the pictures, it doesn't exist!

#15: INVEST IN THE INDIVIDUAL BOTTLES OF SHAMPOO, CONDITIONER, BODY WASH AND MAKEUP WIPES

These basic essentials are something guests have come to expect to be provided when staying at any short-term rental these days. We like to use the individual bottles of shampoo, conditioner, body wash, bar soap and makeup wipes. While slightly more expensive than buying larger containers like you would use at home, having an unopened container for each new guest provides a more sanitary experience. You don't want to leave a guest wondering who was the last to use that big bottle of body wash sitting in the shower.

We don't use the refillable containers mounted on

the wall in the shower because they can get leaky after a while, which means more cleaning for your cleaning crew. Also, sometimes people will be mean and put something other than what's intended in there, believe it or not.

We buy them in bulk from Accent Amenities. We like the starter kits because they come with everything a guest might need. Delivery can take up to two weeks, however, so be prepared for that. You can also buy them in bulk on Amazon as well.

#16: LEAVE AN EXTRA ROLL OF TOILET PAPER ON THE BACK OF THE TOILET

You never know what you have until it's gone. Toilet paper for example.

Leaving an extra roll on the back of the toilet in each bathroom will save guests a trip to the store. One extra roll is typically enough for guests staying 2 to 3 days.

For longer stays, it would be nice to leave a couple of extra rolls in a closet. People will tend to use more if they see there's a lot to spare. So, we just leave 2 to 4 extra rolls for longer stays. But it's entirely up to you and how much you want to spend. Some operators don't leave any at all and some leave 2 rolls per day, which can add up. We tend to provide enough for the maximum number of guests with normal usage for 2 to 3 days.

To be completely transparent with guests, you could write in the description that guests are expected to purchase their own toilet paper after they use what has been supplied.

#17: PROVIDE A KEURIG MACHINE WITH K CUPS, CREAMER, AND MUGS

For coffee-drinkers, life does not start until they have that first or second cup of coffee. Some people drink coffee all day. The Keurig machines are so simple to use nowadays that anyone can do it and you will get few, if any, questions on how to operate it. Mostly because your guests are likely to have one at their own home. They may be more costly than a regular coffee pot, but the returns you will get will far outweigh the upfront expense.

Coffee and creamer are like peanut butter and jelly. You can't have one without the other for most people. It's little touches like providing different flavored creamers for your guests that will make them feel special. You can buy in bulk from Amazon which significantly cuts down on costs.

Oh, and don't forget the mugs.

Pro tip: If you want to go above and beyond, leave a regular coffee pot in a cabinet. Some people will appreciate it.

#18: PROVIDE TEA AND A KETTLE

Not everyone enjoys coffee. Tea is gaining in popularity because of its many health benefits. In this food-centric world, you'll get high praise from guests who aren't coffee drinkers by providing different types of teas and a high-quality kettle.

Get a sampler of different types of teas. For example, provide some herbal tea, green tea, English breakfast tea, Earl Grey tea. Your guests will appreciate having choices.

We cater to families with small children and children get sick. Green tea and tea with peppermint are great choices for anyone with a cold. We place the tea bags in a container and leave it on the counter next to the creamer. The tea kettle is always in an accent color and is left on the stove, partly for decoration as well as functionality.

While the ultimate decision whether to include this item will be determined by your customer and what they want, tea and coffee are fairly universal. We suggest providing both!

#19: USING SOFA BEDS INCREASES CAPACITY

Sofa beds can be the perfect solution to maximize the number of guests that your unit can accommodate. You are likely going to be putting a sofa in anyway so you might as well capitalize on the investment. Sofa beds don't cost that much more than a regular sofa and your return on investment will far outweigh the upfront expense.

One piece of furniture can do double duty as a sofa and a bed, conserving space and money. It's ideal for smaller spaces such as studios or one-bedroom units. But they also work extremely well in larger units. As far as the number of people that you can sleep, it's like adding an extra bedroom.

Plus, let's face it. Kids love sofa beds. Put a kid on a sofa bed and they feel like they are on vacation.

#20: GET RID OF THE CRAPPY MATTRESS THAT COMES WITH THE SOFA BED

Sofa beds are the perfect way to accommodate more guests in your short-term rental. Put them in the living room. Put them in the loft. Put them in the master bedroom if there's enough room. But, please, please, please, replace the crappy mattress that comes with it!

If you've ever slept in a sofa bed, you know how uncomfortable those cheap mattresses can be. Sleeping with a metal bar in your back all night does not make for a good night's sleep. So just replace it. Sell it at the yard sale. Give it to the kids to bounce on. Just get it off the sofa bed.

Replace it with a memory foam one. The memory

foam mattresses available in today's market are durable, affordable, made with high-quality materials and innovative technology. We opt for memory foam because this type of mattress is not too hard and not too soft. They are the most preferred type. Everyone has a different sleeping preference. Memory foam offers medium firmness, sure to please everyone. They also have pressure-relieving benefits according to chiropractors and physicians!

#21: PROVIDE A WASHER AND DRYER IN YOUR UNIT IF AT ALL POSSIBLE

We always look for a washer and dryer that is already in the unit when we do our first walk-through. Most places that we rent come with them. Because we cater to families with children, a washer and dryer are handy because, well, kids are messy. And they wet the bed so it's nice to be able to wash the sheets as they get used, even though we leave out an extra set of sheets for guests for exactly this reason. We know what it's like to have little ones.

It's also nice when guests are staying for an extended period. Most people don't pack a lot of clothes when they travel so being able to wash and dry the few clothes that they brought with them is nice. Someone looking for this will put your listing at the top over other listings that don't supply a washer and dryer.

Use a stackable if space is limited. If your property is short on space, you can still provide them. Stackable units are a great space-saving solution.

Oh, and don't forget the detergent pods.

Pro tip: Don't leave out the entire detergent pod container. Just leave out 3,4 or 5 pods per stay. The container is likely to walk away and that can get costly.

#22: YOUR SUPPLY CLOSET

This advice is primarily for someone operating a single-family home or a townhome, which is what we do. The drawback to this is that we must recreate it every time we get a new unit. If you are planning on operating in apartments or condos, the idea is much the same, just on a larger scale, and you may have one large supply area that serves multiple units in the building. We like to use an entryway closet which is not likely to be used by guests. Plus, it's in a central spot in the home with easy access for the cleaners.

It's also important to note that it should be lockable. If you don't lock it, guests will think that they can use all the items in the closet, and they will! Most closets have a knob with a latch which is easy to install a programmable electronic keypad lock. Simply give the cleaner the access code. If your closet does not have a latch mechanism and opens without turning a knob, purchase a gate lock and a combination padlock. Simply give the cleaner the padlock code.

The supply closet is for the cleaners. It is where all the consumables are stocked such as paper towels, toilet paper, K cups, creamer, trash bags, small trash bags for bathroom trash cans, dishwasher pod containers, laundry detergent pod containers and extra cleaning supplies for cleaners to replenish stock. Purchase a metal 3 shelf storage unit and put all the bulky items at the bottom such as toilet paper and paper towels. Purchase some 3 drawer plastic storage units for smaller items such as extra remotes, batteries, small trash bags, amenities, etc. and label each drawer using a label maker. Place these on the top shelf.

#23: KEEP EXTRA LIGHT BULBS IN THE CABINET ABOVE THE STOVE

This is a short but sweet tip that will save you time and money. It will save you time because you (or your runner) won't have to run out to the unit whenever a lightbulb burns out in the middle of a guest's stay. It's inevitable. It will happen. It will save you money because you won't have to pay someone to do it for you. Guests are usually willing and able to replace a lightbulb in a lamp. However, it gets a little tricky when those hard-to-reach lights go out, like recessed lights in the kitchen or vanity lights in the bathroom. Those are best saved for your maintenance technician or your runner if he/she is handy.

#24: BUY EXTRA BATTERIES

It's inevitable that the smoke detector will start chirping at 3 a.m. in the morning when a guest must get up early for a big business presentation. Trust us. They are not happy about it when that happens. You're not likely to get a stellar review even if the experience has been perfect up until that point. But it's the little things like this that guests will appreciate. So, buy extra batteries. Buy extra batteries for everything; the smoke detectors (ALL of them), TV remotes, the Swiffer mop. Leave them in a drawer in the kitchen or in the supply closet.

While you should develop a schedule for regular

replacement to avoid the need for extras, having them available in the unit is a smart thing to do. They'll be there when you or your guests need them most.

#25: DEVELOP A SYSTEM FOR INVENTORY

An efficient inventory system is indispensable in your business. You're going to need to track your inventory so that you will know what to order and how much. It will also be important to track how much you spend each month on supplies. This is important data that you can use to help you make business decisions.

First you will need a supply closet (See tip #22 Your supply closet). After you have set up your supply closet, you'll need to track everything that goes into it. Below is a list of everything we put in ours:

- Toilet paper
- Paper towels

- Trash bags (Kitchen)

- Trash bags (Bathroom)

- Hand soap

- Dish soap

- K cups

- Creamer

- Amenities

- Laundry detergent pods

- Dishwasher pods

- Sponges

- Tissue boxes

- Windex

We created an Inventory Checklist. This checklist has two columns: ITEM and COUNT. Under the ITEM column, we listed the above items. Under the COUNT column, we made a blank box for each item. Then we printed if off and laminated it. The Inventory Checklist is hung inside the supply closet along with a dry erase marker. Every time our runner comes to the unit, she takes inventory of all the items on the list using the marker. When any item gets below a certain threshold (we use 1), we get notified that the item needs to be reordered.

#26: BUY ODOR ELIMINATOR SPRAY SUCH AS ZEP TO GET OUT CIGARETTE SMOKE

Occasionally, you will have inconsiderate guests who smoke something in your unit. It's a good idea to be prepared for this. Instead of having to call the maintenance technician or the runner to deal with it every time, just leave it in the supply closet for the cleaners. If it's not that bad, Zep will usually take the smell away. But if it's really bad or something other than cigarette smoke, use the ozone machine.

SECTION THREE: TECHNOLOGY AND SECURITY

#27: BUY ROKU SMART TVS

In this section we're going to make a specific suggestion on brand. We use Roku Smart TVs specifically for their ease of use. The remote that comes with a Roku TV is extremely simple and most people have no trouble figuring out how to make it work. As a traveler, it can be very frustrating to show up at a unit with a complicated remote control. Even worse, some setups require multiple remotes.

Make things simple for your guest. Having a very simple remote greatly reduces the amount of times people contact you because they cannot figure out how to work the television. In addition, the Roku interface is very intuitive to most people. Out of the hundreds of guests that have stayed in our units with these TVs and their simple interface and remote, very few have ever asked us how to use them.

#28: PROVIDE USB CHARGERS WHERE GUESTS ARE LIKELY TO CHARGE THEIR PHONES

Nearly everyone has a mobile phone these days. In addition to phones, it's not unusual for guests to travel with tablets, laptops, and other electronic devices that need to be charged.

The nightstands in the bedroom are a prime location to charge devices overnight. Side tables in the living room are another common location for people to want to plugin. USB chargers can be stand-alone units. Even better, consider replacing normal wall outlets with ones that also include USB chargers built in. That way they won't be taken either intentionally or unintentionally by your guests.

Providing dedicated places to charge electronic devices provides a better experience for your guests. It also has another important function. It will deter guests from unplugging your lamps and other items. That will be one less thing that your cleaning crew has to do. It won't stop this from happening every time, but it will cut down on the number of instances. A guest will contact you about a burned-out lightbulb in the bedroom lamp, only to find out that the previous guest unplugged it to charge their phone and tablet. Pro tip: provide bedside lamps with built-in chargers!

#29: INSTALL SMART THERMOSTATS

The biggest advantage for us in using smart thermostats is the ability to remotely control the temperature of the unit. When the unit is vacant, the temperature can be changed to a more efficient temperature, which saves money. For example, if the unit has been vacant for 3 days, we can set the temperature to an energy efficient mode. The morning that a guest is to arrive, we can set it to a more comfortable temperature. This is a nice feature for us.

We prefer the Nest brand thermostats. They are easy for guests to use. Simply turn the knob to the right to make the temperature hotter and left for colder. The temperature is displayed digitally in the center of the device making it easy to read. They also look sleek and modern. Another feature of these thermostats is the ability to control the temperature range. It can be configured so that a guest cannot set a temperature above or below a certain threshold that you have pre-programmed. This can help prevent potential damage to your heating and cooling systems.

#30: USE SMART LOCKS FOR YOUR DOORS

Never provide a physical key! Keys can be copied and can create a security risk. Keys also tend to go missing from time to time, requiring replacement.

Besides the security risks, smart door locks with a code are simply easier for your guests to use. The method for entering the unit will be one of your guest's first impressions of the unit itself. Make that first impression as easy and simple for them as possible.

You should also be able to control your door locks remotely. This is the part that makes them "smart". Typically, they will connect to your wireless network and can be controlled either via a smartphone app or from a computer. A smart door lock will give you the ability to easily change the door code for each new guest. It will also save you when something happens, and a guest cannot get in. You can simply let them in remotely. This also holds true for others that will need access to the unit from time to time such as your cleaners and maintenance crew.

Every member of your team that will need access to the home should have their own code. In this way, assuming your system logs access, you will know who entered and when. In our current system, every door lock has a minimum of seven different codes stored at any given time. The cleaners, maintenance, our runner, two members of management, the current guest, and an additional backup guest code are always stored.

#31: SKIP CABLE AND GO WITH A STREAMING SERVICE

Instead of signing up for cable or satellite consider using a streaming service instead. One of the biggest advantages to this is that it will simplify your remote setup quite a bit. An added advantage is that streaming services can often be split between multiple units. This saves you money over a more traditional setup.

There are many to choose from, but always be thinking ease of use. The easier it is to use, and the more intuitive the service and interface is, the less questions you will get.

#32: USE A DECIBEL MONITORING DEVICE TO MONITOR THE NOISE LEVEL

Installing external cameras is a must. However, having either video or audio recording devices inside your unit is both legally and ethically wrong. So how do you monitor the noise levels to make sure that the guests in your unit aren't playing loud music, yelling, or otherwise causing a nuisance? We use a product called Noiseaware. It is a device that is placed inside the home and monitors sound levels. It does not actually record any sound, but it will tell you how loud any sounds are. You can also monitor this device remotely and have it send you alerts when levels reach a certain threshold.

When there's a potential issue with noise at one of your properties, you will be the first to know. This helps you be a much more responsible neighbor to the community and ensures that you have a backup system to your cameras. Not only will it show you if there are loud noises, it will show you if there are noises at all. A side benefit of this is being able to tell remotely if the property is occupied.

#33: INSTALL EXTERNAL SECURITY CAMERAS

Installing external security cameras is one of the best investments you can make for your short-term rental property. At a minimum, you want at least one camera covering the entrance to your property. A doorbell style camera is ideal for this. If you have additional entrances to your property, you may want to consider covering those as well. If your property has a driveway, we would suggest placing a camera there also.

Having one or multiple external security cameras allows you to have eyes on your property at all times. Even if you were just renting out a room in your home, there are times when you will be away. You need to have a way to monitor your properties when you can't be physically present. Having external security cameras is the solution to this problem.

Security cameras that can be remotely viewed are one of the most important tools that you will have at your disposal. In fact, many of the tips and tricks mentioned in this book simply won't work without them. In addition, many of the horror stories that you hear on the news and from other people could have been prevented had the operator installed security cameras. Security cameras will alert you to the presence of parties, unauthorized guests, and other security concerns.

One word of caution. Never install security cameras in any private area of the unit. In fact, any device that records video or sound should always be installed externally.

#34: TIE IT ALL TOGETHER WITH A SECURITY SYSTEM

We've talked about the importance of utilizing external cameras, smart locks and thermostats. However, having these various systems, although necessary, creates a problem of its own. Each system has its own app, website, password, and username. This creates an inefficiency because they are not integrated with each other. The solution is to tie them all together with one central security system. Not only does this provide one interface to all these systems, it has other advantages as well.

One of the obvious advantages is that you now have a security system. This makes the property more secure when it's vacant between reservations. It's also an amenity that some guests appreciate because it secures their belongings when they are away. It can also help them feel more secure at night when in an unfamiliar city or neighborhood. Beyond the security features, you can now also integrate other important safety devices such as smoke detectors, carbon monoxide detectors and even sensors that can detect water leaks. If an emergency arises, the authorities will automatically be dispatched. If the water heater springs a leak, an integrated water sensor can send an alert before significant damage occurs.

Another advantage to a unified system is that the various components of the system have the ability to communicate with each other. For example, when your security system senses that the property is vacant, you can program it in such a way that the thermostat adjusts to a more efficient temperature. This can lower your operating costs. Another example of how this integration can be beneficial is that it can eliminate single points of failure. Doorbell cameras sometimes fail to detect when a visitor is present. However, you could now program your cameras to automatically record whenever a door is opened. This way, you always get the video clip regardless of whether the camera correctly identifies that a person is present.

Having a security system that ties together all the various components in each one of our units has increased the efficiency and scalability of our business. Not only is it an amenity that we offer to our guests, but it's a critical tool to manage our units.

SECTION FOUR: DESIGN AND PHOTOGRAPHY

#35: DESIGN WITH YOUR PICTURES IN MIND

Great, eye-catching pictures start with great design. Great design starts with great color. Bold colors will make your listing jump off the screen as potential guests are scrolling through a sea of grey and beige. Don't be afraid of color because it will make you stand out and get more clicks. More clicks mean more potential reservations. Your pictures are click-bait.

So, when you start to design your unit, think about what your pictures are going to look like. If you need some inspiration, scroll through some other listings and pick out some pictures that you like. What do you like about it? What makes it stand out to you? It's likely that the color scheme is what caught your eye at first. That's why we say don't be afraid of color.

Visit websites like Pinterest for inspiration as well. Once you've found a color scheme that you like with bold, bright colors, search for designs with that color scheme. We also like to look at the area in which the unit is located. Is it in an arts district? Is it more of an industrial district? Location inspiration is what makes short term rentals so endearing to visitors. Pro tip: Support small, local businesses and use local art on the walls!

Now that you have a great color scheme and inspirational pictures, it's time to put it all together. The first place to start is the art. Great big art. If you have a budget, which you should, put it towards great big canvas art prints or large framed prints and comfy sleeper sofas. A sofa table doesn't need to cost a lot of money, neither do end tables nor lamps. Large art pulls a room together and looks really great in photos. Hang them above the sofa and above the bed.

Bold color scheme, check. Large art, check. We've

already talked about sleeper sofas in tip 14, check. Now all we need are some finishing touches. Throw pillows in contrasting colors will add a beautiful pop of color to your photos. Put them on the sofa and on all the beds. And don't ever forget the lamps. You can't have too many lamps. Put them in the living room, in the kitchen and of course in all the bedrooms.

Pro tip: add an accent wall behind the sofa and the bed for that extra pop of color!

#36: THEME YOUR UNITS. IT WILL MAKE YOU STAND OUT

When we started with our first unit, the theme was already determined. We decided to put the basement of our personal property on Airbnb. Previously, we set it up for ourselves as an in-home movie theatre. We installed an 80-inch screen TV, put in surround sound speakers, and got a big, comfy sofa. We built an entertainment center with a nice rock backsplash. We painted the walls red, then hung our favorite movie posters. When we decided to make it available as a short-term rental, we added a dorm-size fridge, a table, a microwave, a coffee pot and a bed. It was natural for us to list it as a movie theatre experience. Here was our initial description:

You're not in Kansas anymore! Unwind on the recliner sectional sofa or in the California King bed while you enjoy your favorite movie on the 80-inch screen tv with surround sound.

The whole basement floor is yours, including your own private entrance! Convenient to 485 and Charlotte area.

What we didn't realize at the time was how much the theme mattered. People chose to stay with us because of how the unit was themed. We began to see this, not only in their booking requests, but also in their feedback after their stay.

So, when we started adding additional units, we knew choosing a theme would be important. As we've mentioned elsewhere, you're not just providing a place to stay. You are creating an experience. Guests will choose one place over another based on many factors such as location, price, etc., but one thing you may be overlooking is emotion. How does the space make

88 Secrets to Success for Your Short-Term Rental Business

them feel? One of our most popular units is North Carolina themed. This appeals to out-of-state travelers who want the experience of staying in a North Carolina themed unit. It compliments their destination and enhances their experience.

Another one of our most popular units is coffee-house themed. This theme invokes an emotion of the type of experience guests expect to have while staying there. Guests can almost smell the fresh-brewed coffee as they peruse the photos. The best part of waking up in this unit is having a relaxing cup of coffee in a warm, comfortable space.

Theming your units visually and emotionally prepares your guests for the type of experience that they are going to have. This begins the process of them imagining themselves in the space and how it will make them feel. You will stand out to guests who identify with your theme and they may be more likely to book with you.

84

#37: USE BRIGHT, VIVID COLORS ON ACCENT WALLS

An accent, or feature wall, is simply a wall that has a different look to it than all the other walls in the room. It can be a different color, a different texture or a different design. In the short-term rental business, accent walls bring more clicks to your listing. More clicks equal more money.

Most people are so afraid of color that prospective guests are so used to seeing monotone decor as they are searching for a place to book that even a little bit of color in a picture will stand out to them. When a picture stands out, they will click on it.

Accent walls are an easy and inexpensive way to

liven up any space. We already talked about how you should start your design with a great big piece of art. Pick out a bold color from the painting or print that you've chosen. Even if you're keeping your room in a neutral color scheme, a dark brown accent wall will really stand out.

If you want to make a small room appear larger, use green, blue or purple on the accent wall behind the bed. If the room is long and narrow, use warmer colors such as yellow, orange and red on the far end wall to balance out the space.

Don't forget that there's more to accent walls than just paint. You can use tile or stone or wallpaper. Or tile wallpaper. Or stone wallpaper. There really aren't any rules. You can even use shelving or curtains as an accent!

#38: USE COMPLEMENTARY COLORS AS ACCENTS FOR DÉCOR

If we just took the color out of your pallet for using all white linens, don't fret! We've got you covered. Here's a tip you color-courters will love.

Complementary colors are colors that are on opposite ends of the color wheel from each other. Combining two complementary colors together in your design will create high contrast and high impact. When used together, they appear brighter and more prominent. For example, blue and orange or yellow and purple or red and green. One color will be the dominant shade, while the other color will be used as an accent color.

So, here's how to put this together. If your accent wall is red, keep the sofa neutral and use a green hue on the throw pillows. You can also keep the walls neutral and use a blue sofa with orange-hued throw pillows. A mustard yellow accent wall would look stunning with a neutral sofa and purple throw pillows.

Whatever complementary colors you choose, be sure that your art ties them all together.

#39: USE ONLY FAKE GREENERY

Look, it's not the 80's anymore. We no longer need to suffer from the love affair of hideous artificial plants that plagued this decade. Things have changed and faux is SO much better!

If the thought of faux plants has you reminiscing about bright flower boxes and fake flowers planted along sidewalks, it's time to open your eyes to a new world. A world where faux can be just as beautiful as real. If done right, faux can be better than real. So, let's breathe some life into your space, shall we?

In living rooms and bedrooms where there's a bare corner, add a tall 4 or 5 ft tree. Make sure the base pot is sturdy. Big leaf plants such as fig trees go with any decor and really add a punch of color. Any kind of Palm tree, Monster leaf or Lotus leaf plants are also solid choices.

If you have a bookshelf, place a smaller potted faux plant such as a succulent or fern. Ivy also looks great draping down from a top shelf. A coffee table isn't complete without a floral arrangement or small container plant. Tall spiky-leaf grass containers make a great accent piece for the dining room table. And don't forget about the bathroom! Add a pop of color with a floral arrangement in an accent color that coordinates with the room beside it and you're in business.

#40: MOUNT YOUR TVS ON THE WALL

There are a number of reasons why mounting your TVs on the wall instead of using a TV stand is the preferred method for a short-term rental. However, if you look through other operator's pictures on almost any platform, many of them aren't doing it. Here are a few reasons why you should.

For one thing, it looks better in person and in the pictures. For whatever reason, a TV that is mounted on the wall at a proper height for viewing is much more appealing. Is it enough to make the difference in whether someone books your place or not? Probably not by itself, but attention to this type of detail adds up in a potential guest's mind. Often it's not the large things, but a combination of a bunch of small details that make a unit look polished.

Secondly, they are less likely to grow legs and walk off. (It can happen!) Of course, we are talking about theft. Can someone steal your TV even if it is mounted on the wall? Yes, they can, but it does make it more difficult and that might just mean that they don't bother trying.

Another reason to mount your TVs is that you don't have to worry about a guest or their children knocking them over and breaking them. or worse yet, having the TV fall on a person injuring them in the process. We have children and understand completely that parents can't control everything! But even adults can make a mistake and knock an expensive television set off a TV stand. Mounting the TV on the wall doesn't completely eliminate the possibility of damage, but it does reduce the risk greatly.

A quality TV mount can be purchased online for as little as $25. It's a small investment that will not only make your unit look better but be safer as well.

#41: HIDE THE WIRES TO THE TV

So often when browsing the internet looking at other operator's pictures you will see a beautifully decorated unit with a TV mounted on the wall. Everything is done really well and beautifully designed, only to see an ugly black cord hanging from the TV draped down to the wall outlet. Sometimes there are multiple cords. Hiding those cords and wires is a small detail that will make your unit look polished. Not only will it look better in the pictures but in person as well.

Luckily, there is an easy way to fix this. Hiding cords inside the wall is the best solution. Your local hardware store will have inexpensive kits to make this possible. If not available locally, you can also easily find them online. But sometimes that is not an option. In those cases, you can buy cheap plastic raceway that mounts to the surface of the wall. The wires are then run through this to hide them. While the raceway itself is still visible, it still presents a much tidier appearance. Often times it's the small details that matter the most.

#42: CHANGE OUT ALL THE LIGHTBULBS FOR DAYLIGHT BULBS

One of the first things we do when setting up a new unit is to change all the existing light bulbs to daylight bulbs. Here we are talking about color temperature of the bulb, not necessarily the brightness. Many people prefer soft white bulbs in areas such as bedrooms and living rooms because they give a more soft, cozy feel to the space. They tend to give off a more yellowish light than daylight bulbs.

Daylight bulbs are usually preferred in spaces that need a brighter feel such as kitchens and bathrooms. However, when we are setting up a new unit, we are thinking about what is about to happen next. And that very important thing that is about to happen next is our marketing photos. Most everything photographs better with a daylight temperature bulb. That orange puke pleasing glow of the other type of bulb will change the actual color of things in your pictures. That bright white duvet cover will look yellow and dingy. Those clean white walls will also have a yellow tint to them.

So even if you personally prefer soft white or another temperature color of bulb, at least switch out all the bulbs to daylight before your pictures are taken. You can always switch them back to your preferred bulb afterwards. Bonus benefit: Your photographer will thank you!

#43: HIRE A PROFESSIONAL PHOTOGRAPHER, HOPEFULLY ONE THAT SPECIALIZES IN SHORT TERM RENTALS

It is so hard to find a good photographer that knows how to shoot short term rentals. Real estate photography is not the same. You're not trying to sell the house. You're trying to evoke a certain experience through your pictures.

We've gone through three different photographers and we have finally found someone who understands what we're trying to achieve. He was the one that suggested we set the table with all the dishes and glassware. We had never thought about that before. He was also willing to listen to our ideas. We shared photos with him of other listings that we liked. We discussed angle and lighting and equipment.

As he was shooting, we were there. We made sure the pillows were straight and crisp. We made sure the pictures were level. We pulled out the sofa bed and made it up with the comforter, duvet cover, pillows and throw pillows to make it look warm and welcoming. We were there to open the cabinets and drawers in the kitchen to showcase that it is fully stocked. We set the dining room table with all the plates, bowls, glassware and silverware.

All these photos tell the story of the space so that guests can experience it through the pictures.

#44: IF IT'S NOT IN THE PICTURES, IT DOESN'T EXIST

It doesn't exist in the mind of your potential guest anyway. Take pictures of everything in your unit that guests will use or have access to. Yes, I know that you have written it in the listing description, but many people won't read. However, almost everyone will look at the pictures.

Remember that the pictures you provide are a huge part of your marketing. If you provide amenities, show them in the pictures. For example, if the picture of your bathroom doesn't show towels hanging up or folded on a shelf, some people will assume that you don't provide them. If you don't show soap and shampoo, some people will assume they need to bring their own.

If you provide a full kitchen with dishes, glassware, silverware, and other things that are either inside cabinets or drawers, open them and take pictures of what is inside. If you have closets with extra towels and linens, open the doors and show them.

If you provide items that are put away, such as an ironing board or highchair, take a picture of where it is likely to be used. Another great tip is to take a picture of where it is stored. The pictures are not only your marketing, but often they are a guide to current guests as to where items are located.

Doing these things will get you booked more often over your competitors that don't do this for their guests. Another benefit to taking pictures of everything is that potential and current guests won't ask you nearly as many questions. Anything you can do in this business to reduce the amount of time it takes to answer the same questions over and over will ultimately make you more efficient and profitable.

#45: SHOWCASE THE SOFA BED

We've sung the praises of the sofa bed (sofa bed... how do I love thee...let me count the ways). So, you know you need to get them and put them everywhere there's room for one. Now make it a feature!

After the photographer has photographed the space with the sofa as seating, unfold it and make it up nicely with pillows and decorative throw pillows so that the photographer can take a picture of it as a bed. Remember, if it's not in the pictures, it doesn't exist! So, you need to showcase it in your listing photographs.

Make sure that it's made up beautifully. Put pillowcases on the pillows just like guests would do.

Put the comforter on the bed. Then decorate it with the accent throw pillows that you have chosen for your sofa already. (You did remember the throw pillows, didn't you?) Then finish it off with the throw blanket and you're all set for a cozy, beautiful picture that will entice guests to book your place!

#46: SET THE TABLE

Do you remember as a kid getting all dressed up for picture day? Our 8-year-old daughter loves to dress up for picture day. She brushes her own hair which never happens and wants some kind of bow or braid. Our 12-year-old son couldn't care less but when he was little, we always made him wear nice collared shirts and slacks. There's just something about picture day that made you want to look nice. Maybe because you knew the picture was going to be forever.

That's how it should be when the photographer comes to photograph your listing. Your pictures are your number one marketing tool and they need to be perfect. The bed pillows should be straight. The pictures on the wall should be straight. The towels should be even and neat.

When it comes to the dining room, setting the table will create a warm, welcoming photo. It sets the tone and feeling for the space and tells guests "Come, sit down and be together". It lets guests know that you, as the host, think that they are important enough to put in the extra effort for them. It's all about the atmosphere that you are creating for them.

We didn't set the table when we took pictures for our first couple of units. But after hearing about it from our mentors and the new photographer that we hired, we knew we should listen. We're glad we learned about this little tip because it really makes a difference in how our pictures turned out.

Use fake flowers or other fake greenery as a centerpiece (faux is the way to go!). Show enough place settings for the number of guests you claim to host. If your place can host up to 6 guests, show 6 place settings.

Table linens aren't necessary but can provide a pop of color if needed. We like to use table mats for that. Just a basic table setting will do. Use all white dishware. Place the dinner plate a thumb's length from the edge of the table in front of the chair. Put the bowls on top of the plates. To set the table, remember the FORKS acronym. The order is left to right. F is for forks. O is for the plate shape. K is for knife. S is for spoon. I'm not sure what the R is for. The drinking glass goes above the knife. And you're done! Now in your photos, your table will look good enough to eat!

SECTION FIVE: TEAM MEMBERS

#47: YOUR CLEANING CREW CAN MAKE OR BREAK YOUR BUSINESS

The number one thing that will earn you a less than 5-star review is a lack of cleanliness. In other areas of deficiency, a guest may or may not speak up. But when it comes to cleanliness, you are going to hear about it if it isn't top-notch. Perhaps even worse, they won't say anything at all during their stay, but instead leave it in a public review! If you do not deliver high quality consistently in this area, you are doomed to failure.

Look for a cleaner who is detail-oriented. You will also likely need to train them how you want things done. This is not a "set it and forget it" situation. Your cleaning crew is your first line of defense and will be your primary "eyes and ears" when guests check out. They are a critical member of your team.

Your cleaning crew will be the people responsible not only for cleaning, but restaging the unit so it again looks like your marketing pictures. Was the furniture moved? Were decor items rearranged? Was anything damaged? Your cleaners will likely be the first to know!

Take the time to build a relationship with your cleaning crew. When you are just starting out, this may be a single cleaner. That's ok! Give them as much information as you can about how you need things done. Cleaning itself is one thing, but where do the amenities go? How many towels do you provide for each bathroom? How much extra toilet paper do you want to leave out for guests? Be very detailed in the instructions you provide.

Once they have cleaned the unit, follow behind them and see how they did. Provide feedback and repeat until you are getting a consistently clean and thoroughly put back together unit at each turnover.

Remember that they are your partners in this business. The better job they do, the better reviews and the more repeat guests you will receive. This also means more business for them as well. Letting this area of your business slide even a little will kill your future revenue.

#48: HIRE A CLEANING CREW WITH THEIR OWN CLEANING SUPPLIES

Cleaners who come with their own cleaning supplies tend to be more professional. It means they are also acting as a business and this is who you want to hire, a business-minded individual. They will understand the cost of supplies is a business cost for them. They know what it takes to run their business successfully. Why would you risk spending hundreds of dollars on cleaning supplies only to find out that you haven't provided what the cleaner actually needs?

Maybe your unit has hardwood floors, but you forget to supply hardwood floor cleaner. Maybe your unit has granite countertops, but you forget to supply granite countertop cleaner. Maybe your unit has a glass top stove, but you forget to buy glass top stove cleaner. The list is endless. Let the professionals handle it. They will know which brand/kind work best anyway because it is their job to know. Plus, most cleaners like to use their own stuff because they know what to use and how to use it.

You will need to provide some cleaning supplies for your guests, such as Windex, paper towels and some kind of kitchen cleaner like Clorox. You can clean just about anything with just these three items. Leave them under the sink. But for the routine cleaning of a turnover, your cleaners should generally be bringing their own supplies.

Not only will it save you from having to purchase all these things, it will save space in your supply closet. You may think it's cheaper to buy your own cleaning supplies and pay your cleaner less. But is it really cheaper? Think about all the time you spend ordering those supplies. What is your time worth? And who takes the supplies to the unit? You? Someone else?

Don't you have to pay that person to do that for you?
You'll find that it's cheaper in the long run to have the
cleaner supply their own cleaning supplies.

#49: TAKE THE TIME TO FIND AT LEAST TWO DEPENDABLE CLEANERS

We've already talked about how critical good cleaners are to your business and the importance of training them well. It's also important that you find and train more than one. Even if one of your "cleaners" is an entire company with multiple employees, this still represents a single point of failure. You never want that in one of your core operations.

Use one cleaner as your primary cleaner and the second as the backup cleaner for each property. Having a backup cleaner will help ensure that each turnover goes smoothly and is completed on schedule. It also gives you peace of mind. Even if you have the best, most reliable cleaning company, things still happen. Perhaps there is a glitch in your software and your cleaner doesn't get notified that a cleaning needs to be done. Or maybe the cleaning company is training a new cleaner, they do a terrible job, and they cannot return in time to fix the problem before the next guest arrives. Cleaners are people too, and sometimes they fall ill. Then, there are holidays to work around.

Some key questions to ask are:

- How often are your cleaners available?
- How much advance notice do they need?
- How many clients do you have? Does this impact your availability?

Even with these questions answered, make sure you have a backup. You will eventually need them.

#50: DON'T BE AFRAID TO TRY MANY DIFFERENT CLEANERS UNTIL YOU FIND "THE ONE"

Short term rental cleaning is tricky and there is no standard for cleaners. But some are better than others. Some understand the business, and some don't. That's why it's so important to train your cleaners as to what you expect from them. But with that said, if you are not getting the quality that you need or the cleaning crew isn't improving to meet your standards, don't be afraid to look elsewhere and hire a different crew.

Most professional cleaners in general will be able to clean a puke stain or know the best way to clean granite countertops. Therefore, rule number one is to hire professionals. Don't hire your best friend or any friend or any friend of a friend. Hire a professional and hopefully a professional company that can accommodate last-minute requests. If your friend is not doing a good job, that relationship can get strained very quickly. It's better that you don't put yourself in that situation.

Unless you get extremely lucky on the first try, you are likely going to be replacing your cleaning crew at some point. Don't hesitate to replace them. You must have confidence in the ability to trust that the unit will be turned over properly every time. Providing your guests with a clean unit, especially bathrooms and kitchens, is vital to your success. A bad experience in this area not only affects the guests that encounter the problem, sometimes requiring you to refund monies, but an unfavorable review affects your future ability to attract quality bookings as well.

#51: HIRE A PROFESSIONAL LAUNDRY SERVICE TO CLEAN AND BLEACH YOUR LINENS

Hiring a professional laundry service to clean and bleach your linens will save you time and money. They have well-trained, experienced professionals who are knowledgeable in removing dirt and tough stains using the right products and efficient machines.

Their machines can handle larger loads which is more efficient than you or your cleaner could ever be. These machines will also take better care of the linens making them last longer which saves you money.

Turn around is usually the next day and most offer a drop-off and pick up service. These professionals even know how to fold a fitted sheet! Your linens will come back folded perfectly every time so your cleaners will not have to worry about it.

When we first started, we did what a lot of people do, and had our cleaning crew do the laundry in the unit. What we soon discovered, however, was that this method wasn't very scalable. Once you get to the point where you have multiple units, the time available to get them all cleaned in one day becomes limited. In addition to that, we were paying more for the cleaning overall than we would have by letting the laundry people do the job that they were really good at, and let the cleaning people do the job they were experts at, which was primarily cleaning. Since we started doing it that way, costs have gone down and quality has gone up.

#52: HIRE A RUNNER

Many things can be remotely managed, but there are going to be times when a visit to the property is necessary. There are scheduled tasks such as restocking inventory, taking the trash to the curb, and changing filters. However, there are some unscheduled tasks that need to be performed as well, such as changing batteries in a beeping smoke detector, or resetting the modem when the wifi stops working. This is an important position so find someone with integrity. This person will have access to all your properties, including all your supply closets. They will also occasionally interact with your guests.

We also utilize our runner for every check out. Many times, she is first on the scene when a guest departs. Sometimes, she even must tactfully remind guests that check out is at 11 AM in case they "forget". She is responsible for picking up the clean linens at the laundry service and taking them to the units, making sure the cleaners have what they need to make up all the beds and hang all the towels. She then takes inventory of all the consumables in the supply closet such as toilet paper, paper towels and K-Cups. When stock is low, she notifies us and refills as necessary.

The runner is intimately familiar with each unit, what it is supposed to look like, and what is supposed to be in it. At each checkout, the runner assesses the condition of the property and notifies us if something is broken, damaged or missing. She also reports situations that require special attention, such as someone smoked in the unit. The runner documents any discrepancies by taking pictures. She also takes pictures of our more valuable items to ensure that we have a record of their existence should they go missing.

Although some of the runner's tasks overlap with the cleaner's job, we like for the runner to check it as well. This extra set of eyes helps to ensure that nothing is missed, like dead batteries in the TV remote or leftover food in the refrigerator. As an additional benefit, we have a report of how the unit was left, which helps us to leave an accurate review for our guests.

The runner position is a critical one, and that person will have many tasks. In the beginning, you may be the runner for your business, but over time you'll need someone else to take over. This should be one of the first positions that you fill.

#53: DEVELOP A RELATIONSHIP WITH YOUR LANDLORD OR PROPERTY MANAGER

We have acquired most of our units thus far by simply renting them from an existing landlord and repurposing them as short-term rentals. This tip is for those of you following the same business model or those that wish to. It's also useful for current landlords who are considering leasing their long-term units to a professional operator.

Your relationship with your landlord or Property Manager is much like a partnership, just as it is with your cleaners. You need to be someone they know, like and trust. Trust begins by establishing upfront what will happen in case something goes wrong. What if the roof leaks? What if the AC goes out? What if a light bulb goes out? Discussing who will be responsible for what in the beginning will save you a lot of headaches later when things do go wrong.

This business, like most businesses, is all about relationships. This is where it's important to know your business, inside and out because you will need to be able to explain it to him/her. Be business minded. Think like a business owner. Act like a business owner. Talk like a business owner. Because that's who you are-a short term rental business owner. He or She is also a business owner and will appreciate being able to relate to you in that way.

Be able to explain the value that you bring to him or her as well as to the marketplace.

#54: MAINTENANCE ISSUES ARE A PARTNERSHIP BETWEEN YOU AND YOUR LANDLORD OR PROPERTY MANAGER

If you are following the same business model that we are currently using with most of our units, then you will have a landlord or property manager. One of the best parts of our value proposition as a professional operator is that we handle (and pay for) most minor maintenance.

Mostly this is out of necessity. We generally have guests checking out at 11 AM and new guests arriving at 4 PM. This gives us just five hours to clean, replenish any supplies, and do any needed maintenance. Arriving guests expect the unit to look just like the pictures did and they also expect everything to be working. So, if there is a clogged toilet, we are the ones unclogging it. If a cabinet door has come off its hinges, we are making the repair. If the paint needs a touch-up, we are the ones in there with a paintbrush.

While minor maintenance isn't something that we bother the landlord with, there are times that something more major happens. In those cases, the repair is out of our scope as operators so far as paying for it goes. This is where things can get more complicated if you haven't taken the time to discuss these things with your landlord or property manager up front. Remember, they are really partnering with you in this business. Their success is at least in part tied to yours. And your success is partly tied to theirs. Your ability to provide a quality experience to your guests will greatly impact whether this location or unit is profitable or not. And that profitability will be a big part of the decision for you as an operator to either renew the lease at the end of the term or end that arrangement and move on to a more promising unit.

Repairs to major systems, and how well and timely they are performed, fall into this category of mutual success or failure.

For example, over the summer we had a central air conditioning unit at one of our properties stop working during a guest's stay. The guest reached out to us at 10 PM one evening to tell us that the unit had stopped working and they had an elderly family member staying with them. This is a real emergency in North Carolina when it is 100 degrees Fahrenheit during the day and in the 80's, even at night. We knew that this wasn't something that we were responsible for financially, however, we could not get ahold of our landlord very quickly at that time of night, and waiting for a response to the situation was a stressful place to be in. Short term guests do not think as long term tenants would. They want it fixed NOW, and they often want refunds of monies paid if it isn't fixed right away.

So, to save our reputation and the reservation, we took it upon ourselves to call a 24/7 big box repair place who was willing to come on short notice. It was a very expensive repair and we ended up eating the cost. Even worse, they did not end up fixing the problem properly and the very next day the same thing happened again! SO, we sent out yet another big company to fix the new problem. At this point, our guests were very upset with the situation and we ultimately ended up providing them a refund for their stay of a few days. So not only were we out the cost of the repairs, we lost the revenue from the reservation as well. Combined, this was over $2500 lost in just a few days.

Something needed to be done, so we explained what had happened with our landlord. Remember that you are partners in many ways, so they may have ideas and solutions as well. What we decided to do going forward was to come up with a list of preferred vendors for every major thing that we could think of. Plumbing, electrical, HVAC, roof leaks, etc. Now we could call those vendors directly and the landlord would feel confident in the pricing and quality and pick up the repair bills if we had to act on short notice.

So, a few weeks later, the same situation happened at a different location that we had with the same landlord. This time, we had an entire HVAC unit replaced within 24 hours, the landlord loaned us his portable air conditioning units to keep the guests comfortable overnight, and we received a five-star review from the guest! What a difference it made being on the same team and having those conversations in advance.

Since that time, we've taken the lead on helping our landlords handle quite a few repairs. On one occasion, a tree fell onto the electric wires running into one of our units. This not only knocked out the power, but it did some roof damage, knocked off a section of gutter, and bent the service mast for the electric that protrudes from the roof. Our landlord was out of town on vacation! But because we already had an agreed-upon vendor list and an attitude of partnership, we were able to remove the tree, repair the gutters, get permits for the repairs from the city, coordinate the electrician and have everything back up and running in a day. And not just any day, this happened on July 3rd. One day before a major holiday.

Remember it's not just about what is in the lease about who pays for what. It's the when and how that matters, perhaps even more in the short-term rental business.

#55: HIRE A BOOKKEEPER THAT SPECIALIZES IN SHORT TERM RENTALS

Your bookkeeper is one of the most important members of your team. Consider for a moment a scenario like this:

It's the beginning of April. Taxes are due in fifteen days. You haven't touched the QuickBooks accounting spreadsheet for six months because you hate doing it. Plus, you have no idea what you're doing so you're making it up as you go along. Where did you put that receipt for that sofa you bought a couple of months ago? Oh, here it is in this drawer with all the other receipts. Oh my! That's a big stack of receipts you have there. Now how long is it going to take you to go through that whole stack of receipts? Are you really saving money by doing this yourself? The answer is NO!

Your time as a business owner should be devoted to growing your business, developing marketing strategies, securing funding, and other key areas of daily operation. Even if you have a background in finance, or even a working knowledge of accounts payable, accounts receivable and taxes, it's better to let a trained and certified professional handle this aspect of your business.

But don't hire just any ol' bookkeeper. A successful short-term rental business requires specific data to measure performance, attract investors, and for general peace of mind. Your bookkeeper should understand the special requirements of the short-term rental business. For example, suppose you receive a payout from Airbnb to your company bank account. This single payment may represent multiple transactions including the nightly rate, early check-in fees, cleaning fees, management fees, and more. To make it even more complicated, this one payment may represent a combined payout from multiple properties. And you must consider the expenses that were deducted from your payout, such as service fees, commissions, and merchant fees. The sheer number of accounting entries required to record this one deposit could be overwhelming. And that's just one deposit! As a short-term rental owner, you need to know not only from which property income is derived, but which category it fits into. For example, how much of your income is derived from your cleaning fee? How much is from early check-in fees? How much of that came from your linen fee? You also need to know your total expenses and what category they fit into. How much are you spending on linens per turnover, for example? How much is the platform costing you? What are you spending on utilities? This will help you answer key questions; are you charging enough for cleaning? Is your linen fee too high or too low? How low can your nightly rates be and still make a profit? Ultimately, your bookkeeper's job is to not only balance the books, but also to organize your financial data in such a way that the information is relevant to your specific business. If you're looking for a recommendation, the company we use for our bookkeeping is Organized Gains out of California. They specialize in short-term rental bookkeeping. Look them up and be sure to tell them John and Wynde Williams sent you!

Your bookkeeper will keep your books in order and run reports showing how you are doing financially each month. This is invaluable data. It will help you make key business decisions and add a layer of legitimacy to your numbers. Just make sure you choose someone who understands your specific business needs.

#56: GET INSURANCE SPECIFICALLY FOR SHORT-TERM RENTALS. YOUR REGULAR INSURANCE PROBABLY WON'T COVER EVERYTHING.

Insurance is one of those things that most people don't think about until they need it. By that time, it's too late. Never assume that whatever coverage your rental platform is providing is actually insurance because it's usually not. A typical homeowner's policy or even a landlord policy usually doesn't cover your possessions or liability while your property is being occupied by a guest.

Having a conversation with your insurance professional is vital to making sure that you are actually covered in the event of a worst-case scenario. For example, suppose a guest leaves and takes your television with them. Are you covered? Suppose you have a guest that slips and falls in the bathtub injuring themselves. Are you covered in that situation? Running a short-term rental business may bring with it additional liability over what a typical landlord might face.

It may turn out after speaking with your insurance professional that all you really need is an additional endorsement to your existing policy. Or, you may discover that you need an entirely different insurance product all together. There are companies out there that specialize in vacation and short-term rentals. If you are in doubt, search for them online and contact each one to see what they provide and what kind of coverage they offer.

Insurance is one of those areas where you don't want to mess around. Finding out after the fact that you weren't covered or that you were underinsured can be devastating to your business. So, take it seriously. Invest the time in locating a quality insurance policy that covers your specific business. It's one of the first things that you should do!

#57: USE A PEST CONTROL COMPANY BECAUSE THERE WILL BE BUGS!

Bugs are everywhere. They just are. We've got one place with a nice back deck and shady, fenced-in backyard but the mosquitoes are ruthless out there. We want our guests to be able to enjoy the entire space, so we hired a pest control company.

We have neither the time nor the know-how to be able to solve pest problems and safely apply the appropriate solutions. Which is why we hire a professional company to do it for us. They also have access to more effective products and tools that are not available in stores to regular consumers. Some pest problems require special treatment and specialty equipment.

Here in the South, we call roaches Palmetto bugs but they're HUGE. If you've never seen one, you're in for a real treat! They live in trees and fly around, but they don't usually come in the house unless you leave food out or leave the door open. We had some guests stay with us for about 3 months because their house got flooded from a leaky dishwasher. They decided to remodel and needed a place to stay for a couple of months. So, they moved in to one of our houses. It wasn't long before they messaged us about some roaches (aka Palmetto bugs). We sent our pest guy out there and come to find out, they would leave the back door open while sitting on the back porch at night, enjoying some after-work cocktails and those buggers would just fly right in.

SECTION SIX: OPERATING YOUR BUSINESS

#58: AUTOMATE MESSAGING AS MUCH AS POSSIBLE

Messaging with guests is a core activity in the short-term rental business. It's also one of the most time-consuming aspects of the business. For example, in our system, every reservation requires at least five, and as many as seven different messages. We send one message when a potential guest inquires about a unit. A second message is sent when the guest books their reservation. A third message is sent close to their arrival with check in instructions. A fourth message is sent on the day of their arrival informing them of their unique door code. A fifth message is sent during their stay to ensure all is well. A sixth message is sent prior to their departure with their check out instructions. And finally, a number of days after a guest departs, we send them a final message requesting a review. And that's if they don't ask any questions! Once you grow beyond one or two units, the sheer volume of messaging that is required can become overwhelming and take up most of your time, not to mention feeling repetitive.

On some platforms, if you don't respond within a certain amount of time, you will go down in the rankings. What happens if a guest messages you at 2 AM? Fortunately, there are software tools that will allow you to automate your repetitive messaging. Booking.com, for example, has this functionality built into their platform. Sometimes this functionality is built into property management software designed specifically for short term and vacation rentals. We prefer a product named SmartBnB. It's specifically designed to automate messaging on several major platforms. We chose this tool because of the level of customization it allows. It also has the ability to answer frequent questions. The only drawback is that it does not facilitate messaging on every platform that we use for marketing, including our direct bookings. For those channels, we utilize a combination of property management software and built-in platform tools.

Eliminating the human element from your messaging completely isn't possible. There will be times when a guest asks a question to which a human response is required. However, the more you can automate your responses, the lower your expenditures in both time and money will be. Automation will allow you to scale to more units while having a smaller team. It brings efficiency and consistency to your messaging system, and ultimately should be a part of every successful short-term rental business.

#59: USE AUTOMATED PRICING SOFTWARE

Revenue management is a key component to your business. You must be constantly working to ensure that your pricing is optimized. There are many different variables that go into this. Seasonality, local demand, and even the day of the week are things to take into consideration. Keeping up with all of these variables on your own can be a challenge, especially when you have multiple units.

Automated pricing software can assist you in dynamically adjusting your nightly prices as conditions change. Remember, however, that pricing software is just a tool. You will still have to provide some input based on your own expenses and how aggressive your strategy is. Nonetheless, having an automated tool that can adjust nightly pricing based on hundreds of variables is invaluable. If you are overpriced for certain nights, you may be facing vacancy issues. Conversely, if you are underpriced, vacancy may not be a problem, but profitability will suffer.

Two of our favorite pricing tools are available online. Pricelabs is one of them and Wheelhouse is the other. They each have their own strengths and weaknesses, but both are better than trying to do it yourself manually.

#60: MONITOR SECURITY CAMERAS AS GUESTS CHECK IN

If you're following the advice to have external security cameras installed at each one of your units, then you will be able to follow this one as well. At every check-in, put a system in place to verify that guests have arrived. It should become part of your process to check that the guests arriving match what was disclosed in the booking. For example, is the number of guests correct? Do the guests that are arriving match the description of the person that made the booking? Are they bringing in extra items that may be of concern? It's always better to head off any potential problems right away.

Every day at check-in time we monitor the cameras at each property to verify that guests have checked in and all appears well. If the guest has not yet arrived, we keep checking back at regular intervals until they do. Consider setting a regular schedule for this and having a way to track it electronically. This will set you up for success later and allow you to pass this task along to a virtual assistant.

#61: CHANGE DOOR CODES IN BETWEEN GUESTS

Changing door codes in between guests provides an additional level of security. If you are always using the same code, that code can be shared, just like keys can be copied. Internet-connected smart locks can replace your existing deadbolt with a keypad feature. With the keypad feature, you get the ability to create access codes that can be changed remotely. You don't even need to be physically at the property. It's all online!

It can also be a way to improve the experience for your guests. Consider setting the code to something that is personal to them and that they can easily remember. Using the last four digits of their phone number can be a great way to accomplish this.

#62: HAVE A CHECKLIST FOR YOUR CLEANERS

When the cleaners come to clean your unit for the first time, they will not know what to expect. Lay it all out for them. It's important to list out all the duties that you expect them to do for you.

Make your checklist while you are at the unit or at least take pictures of every single room. It's much easier than trying to remember where exactly the towel rack is or where the creamer goes from memory.

Start at the beginning. Provide the cleaners with the address to the property, where they should park and how to access the property. Document all of this on your checklist. Put it at the very top and label it as

IMPORTANT INFO (or something similar).

IMPORTANT INFO

- *Property address is 5 Star Street, Charlotte, NC 28205*
- *Please park in the parking spot in front of the house. If this spot is not available, please park in any marked parking spots along the street.*
- *The code to get in is 1234*
- *The supply closet is located in the entryway closet. The code to the lock is 5678.*

The next section of the checklist should be the room that the cleaners will enter when they first walk in the door. If it's the living room, start with the living room. Label your checklist by room. It will look something like this:

LIVING ROOM

- *Dust all furniture*
- *Clean crumbs/spills from sofa*
- *Clean windowsills*

- *Vacuum floor and rug*

Provide pictures of what the unit should look like. Use your marketing pictures if you have them available. This will help the cleaners tremendously and you will not get nearly as many calls or emails back and forth about where to put a fuzzy blanket.

#63: DO QUALITY CONTROL

In the hospitality industry, exceeding guest expectations is our goal. We go above and beyond to make sure they have a 5-star experience in any of our units. They expect the best, therefore, we expect our contractors (cleaners, runners, maintenance crew) to be the best every single time they do work for us. The quality of their work is essential to building our business, as it will be with building your business. The better job the cleaners do, the better our reviews. The better reviews we get, the more business we get. The more business we get, the more business the cleaners will get.

But not everyone is consistently good. People have good days and bad days. It is our responsibility as business owners to see to it that our units are consistently cleaned well. Our guests deserve it and our business depends on it. In order to maintain our high-quality standards, we need to have someone check behind the cleaners randomly to make sure they are providing a 5-star experience for our guests.

Sometimes, we are the ones who check behind the cleaners. Sometimes, it's the Runner. If we have something to take care of at one of the units such as fixing the Wi-Fi, we will also look to see how well the cleaners have done their job. We take pictures of anything that is not up to our standards. Then we notify the cleaning company, providing them with evidence of what we have found. We then expect it to be fixed.

Just recently, we had to fire one of our cleaning companies. We had a guest complain that the unit was not clean, so we started checking after the cleaning crew each time they cleaned this unit. 2 times out of 3, the unit was not even cleaned. The toilets were not cleaned. We found hair in the shower stall. There were no towels hung up. They even left bars of soap on the side of the tub! Can you imagine if a guest had checked-in that day??!! Horrific. You're fired.

#64: DEVELOP A SYSTEM FOR YOUR LINENS

When we first started, we were having the cleaners wash, dry, fold and put away all the sheets and towels. It took them hours to clean just one unit. We thought "How are we going to scale this?". What are we going to do when we have 10 units? What about 50? Are we going to hire one cleaning crew for each unit? It didn't seem logical or scalable, so we had to come up with a solution.

Then we discovered laundry services. But not just any laundry service would do. They had to have the big load washers and dryers and they had to have the manpower to do all the linens for us. If every bed is used and every towel is used in one unit, it adds up to 20 pounds of laundry. Plus, it all needs to be bleached.

So, we shopped around. We thought about hiring a service that would come pick up the linens, wash them, and bring them back but that was too expensive. It also presented logistical problems with our single-family units. We visited a few laundry service providers and asked if they had what we needed. We finally found one.

It didn't look like much on the outside; old, kind of small, but inside it was perfect. We were greeted by the owner that day. He just happened to be in the store doing some bookkeeping. We explained what we needed, and he said he could help us out. He even offered to let us use one of the back rooms to store the linens until we could pick them up. And he gave us a key. It was the perfect solution for us.

Now the problem became how are we going to get the dirty linens there and get the clean linens back to the unit? The Runner! The Runner can pick up the clean linens and take them to the unit. While she's there at the unit, she can strip the beds and take away all the dirty linens in the color-coded bags and drop them back off at the laundry servicer. It's the perfect solution!

#65: HAVE A ROBUST SET OF HOUSE RULES AND ENFORCE THEM

Early on in our business, we had very few written house rules. We assumed wrongly that many things should be common sense. Unfortunately, common sense is not all that common and you should never assume anything. A clearly defined set of house rules is essential and sets expectations for guests.

The first time we realized that we needed to make changes in this area occurred one Saturday night just a few months into our foray into the short-term rental business. At this time, we were still operating as amateurs and weren't even thinking about having multiple units. We had just gotten the idea to put our basement on Airbnb to make a few bucks and help us pay the mortgage. It all started with a one-night-stay inquiry from a potential guest who wanted to know if age was an issue. While this seemed a little curious and should have been a red flag, we simply did not have the experience at the time to know any better. We responded that no, age was not an issue as long as the house rules were not violated. At that time, we had very few actual house rules in place. Only basic things like no smoking, no pets, and no parties or events made the initial list. On the night the guest was scheduled to arrive, we had taken the kids to the movies. As we approached the house on our way back home, we noticed a large number of cars parked along the street. One of us made the comment to the other "Somebody must be having a party. I wonder who it is". It wasn't until we pulled into the driveway that we realized that person was us! Upon inquiring with the guest, we discovered that not only were the four people that were on the reservation there, but they had invited no less than 25 of their closest friends to "hang out". The music was loud and there were way more people in the space than should have been. At this point, we should have ended the reservation immediately and removed everyone from the property. However, we were still relatively new and inexperienced. Instead of enforcing compliance, our reaction was more along the lines of complaining. The guests did not respond to our complaints and, even though we were able to turn away even more visitors as they arrived, most of the ones who were initially there stayed. Imagine the mess they left! Peach Schnapps was on the carpet. All the shot glasses were used and left everywhere, even in the couch. There was trash all over the place. We learned our lesson the hard way. Here's where we went wrong. We didn't have a complete set of house rules; we had no age restrictions, we allowed a one-night stay on a weekend, we did not have a clear definition of who was a guest vs who was a visitor, we did not have a rule stating maximum occupancy, and we did not have defined quiet hours. These are just a few of the house rules we have added since. The one house rule that we DID have against parties, we didn't properly enforce. We failed to demand compliance or provide a consequence for noncompliance. The result of our failure was a larger than normal cleaning bill, an annoyance created not only for ourselves but also our neighbors, and an elevated risk of liability.

Since that time, we've strengthened our house rules and learned the importance of monitoring for compliance. We recently had a reservation at one of our townhome units that was for 8 people. The guests initially arrived with 9 people and, over the course of the next few hours, even more visitors arrived, totaling 17 in all. Our house rules now include a maximum occupancy limit not to exceed the number of guests that the unit can accommodate. We also have defined the difference between a visitor and a guest. A guest is a person who stays overnight in the unit and should be stated on the reservation. A visitor is someone who comes and goes. Visitors should not stay past 10 PM and are included in the maximum occupancy calculation at all times. A visitor becomes a guest when he or she stays past 10 PM. At this point, this reservation was in violation of both of these rules. We took swift action to communicate with the guest and informed them of which rules they were violating. We then gave them a chance to comply by a set time or face cancelation of their reservation and removal from the property. In this case, the guests did comply and the remainder of the stay was uneventful.

Having a robust set of house rules and, perhaps even more importantly, enforcing them quickly, will greatly reduce the number of problems that you face. Your house rules help to set clear expectations for guest's behavior. Put in place a clear set of rules, monitor for compliance, and enforce them when they are violated.

#66: HAVE AN SOP (STANDARD OPERATING PROCEDURE) FOR EVERYTHING!

You're not going to be cleaning your units yourself. You're not going to be repairing things yourself. You're not going to be messaging guests yourself (maybe at first, but not forever). Start thinking of yourself as a business owner. Business owners tell others what needs to be done and how things need to be done. So, you, as the business owner, need to document the what and the how of everything you do.

We did do everything ourselves at first, but we quickly realized that was not scalable. We cannot clean all our units ourselves. Therefore, it was important for us to hire a cleaning company. But they didn't know what the unit was supposed to look like or how we wanted it cleaned. We had to document all this information so that the cleaners would know. That's how our Cleaning Checklist was developed, for example.

Having standard procedures in place for every situation is being proactive rather than reactive. Every time you find your business in a new situation, or with a problem that you haven't encountered before, document how you handled it (or should have handled it) and make that your standard procedure for next time the situation arises. Over time, you will develop a robust and thorough set of SOPs. Stick to them! Even if you are the one implementing them at first, treat them the way you would want an employee to do so.

#67: DOCUMENT EVERYTHING!

You spend so much time in the beginning designing your business, coming up with ideas for your business and implementing systems and processes in your business. It would be a shame to lose all that work if something were to happen. So, write it down. Write down everything that you do and how you do it. Put it in a Google Doc or whatever makes sense for you. Just take the time and do it. If you start out doing it from the very beginning, it will become a habit which you won't regret. We wish we had someone to tell us this in the beginning which is why we are telling you. Don't make the same mistake we did. There are two main reasons we learned why documentation is so important.

First, when one of us went away or got sick, we had no idea what the other one was doing or how they were doing it. We each have certain aspects of the business that we oversee. John does all the tech stuff, messaging, data reports and much, much more. Wynde oversees design, inventory and personnel and that's about it. John does everything else. And so, it will be with your business. Everybody will have certain tasks that they are responsible for doing. You need to document all the instructions and goals so that person knows exactly what he or she is supposed to do and how to do it. It will save you from having to repeat yourself over and over. Sometimes, we make videos on how to do things. Plus, if that person ever leaves, you can just plug someone else into that task and voila!

Documentation also allows you to organize your systems and processes more consistently. Systems and processes are at the core of your business. For example, we document how to respond to all types of messages that we get from guests and potential guests. Instead of reinventing the wheel every time a guest asks about how far away the unit is from some place or parking or discounts, document what you say and then use it every time. That way it doesn't matter who's doing it. It's the same every time. It's consistent.

SECTION SEVEN: REVENUE AND CALENDAR MANAGEMENT

#68: OFFER AN EARLY CHECK-IN FOR A FEE

The short-term rental business isn't necessarily one of occupancies. One of the keys to being profitable is not to solely focus on price per night and how many nights per month are occupied. This is a revenue business. Finding ways to offer extra value to your guests that you can charge for boosts your bottom line.

One of the easiest things to do is to offer early check-ins. With each reservation that comes in, if the night before is not booked, offer the guest the option to early check-in for a fee. What you charge is up to you, but, in general, we will block off the previous night to accommodate their early arrival. For us, guests check out at 11:00 am and new guests check-in at 4:00 pm. In order to accommodate an early arrival without blocking off the previous night, we would need to contact the cleaners, message the staff, rearrange schedules, need confirmation that schedules can be rearranged, etc. While this is doable with a small number of units, imagine the nightmare that this would become with dozens of units!

Our advice is to keep it simple. Only offer this option when the previous night is available. All that requires is that you block off the previous night on your calendar and charge an appropriate amount that makes it worth your while to do so.

You normally want to charge at least as much as what the previous night is costing you. This strategy works especially well if the previous night is one that is likely to be vacant anyway. Someone books a stay starting on a Thursday, for example, and stays through Monday. The Wednesday before, if not already booked, has a lower chance of being reserved simply because it's a Wednesday. Combine that with a previous reservation that ends on a Tuesday. Now you have an orphan night in the middle of the week. The likelihood of an orphan day in the middle of the week getting booked is even lower. So why not offer your guest the option to check in early and recapture the cost of that lost night?

#69: OFFER A LATE CHECK OUT FOR A FEE (MAYBE)

Much like offering an early check-in for a fee, offering a late checkout can also be a way to earn extra revenue. This one, however, presents unique challenges. The main problem that you will encounter is that most people won't pay for them ahead of time. Early check-in, even if you don't make the initial offer, is asked for much more often. In addition, you usually have enough advance notice to know whether the previous night is open or not. We suggested earlier that blocking off the previous night is the best practice for accommodating an early check-in.

Late checkouts on the other hand are usually

requested either the night before a guest is leaving or the morning of a guest departure. The problem with this is that even if no other guest is checking in that day, the wheels are already in motion for your cleaning crew to arrive at checkout time. In our system, the runner is scheduled to arrive as well. You might even have scheduled maintenance that day! Making the calls to these various vendors and staff asking them to alter their schedules at the last minute is an extra expense in time, a loss in efficiency, and generally annoying to your team members.

For those reasons, we generally make it our policy to not allow late checkouts. The only exception to this is when a guest happens to request it far enough in advance that we can block off the following night. This way the cleaning crew and our staff will simply plan to arrive the next day and all is well.

Also keep in mind that as you scale, it will become more and more difficult to keep track of who wants a late checkout vs who wants an early check-in. Those two things cannot generally happen on the same day in the same unit. Given the added complexity of offering both options, you may find that it makes more sense to just never allow late checkouts and instead focus solely on early check-ins as an additional revenue source. Nevertheless, there is an opportunity there to bring in additional revenue. Ultimately, it's up to you as the operator to decide if it's worth the extra scheduling hassles to make it profitable.

#70: MAKE SURE NO ONE IS CHECKING IN OR OUT ON A MAJOR HOLIDAY

Your team members become like family and you want to take good care of them. Allowing them to spend time with their families on major holidays such as Easter, Christmas, New Years and Thanksgiving shows that you care about them and value them. It's a must in order the gain and attract quality help.

Fourth of July can be a tricky one, but we usually don't have any problems getting the cleaners to come since they work during the day and most festivities don't happen until that evening. But it's something for you to think about as you are creating your business.

#71: IF YOU DON'T HAVE CARPET, THINK ABOUT MAKING YOUR UNIT PET-FRIENDLY. IT'S A MONEY-MAKER!

People traveling with their pets has become a HUGE market. Why not tap into some of that business yourself? In most cases, a pet-friendly unit can command a premium over those units that do not allow pets. You may be able to get as much as 20% to 30% more by making your unit pet-friendly. There's money to be made, but there are some things to consider before you begin serving this type of guest.

Don't have carpet. Don't have carpet anywhere. Even if it's just in the bedrooms, there's potential for accidents and fleas. You don't want to have to drag out the carpet steamer or spot cleaner when accidents happen. And fleas love carpet.

Pet-friendly units require more cleaning. If you have dogs like we do, you know what I'm talking about. We have two 100-pound labs that shed enough to make a blanket daily. And they get on the furniture. You can get one of those Sofa Shields to put on the sofa which can go to the cleaners. Make sure to put on your Cleaning Checklist for the cleaning crew to vacuum the sofa every time. You'll also need to change the filters out at least once a month.

Make it very clear in your listing that your unit is pet-friendly as some people are sensitive to pet hair. This also helps those looking for pet-friendly units find you.

#72: USE A CENTRAL CALENDAR TO PREVENT DOUBLE-BOOKINGS

You can list your unit on multiple platforms such as Airbnb, VRBO/HomeAway, and Booking.com, but remember that each platform has its own calendar. If you have your units listed on multiple platforms, you will need a way to sync them all together. For example, if someone books your unit on Airbnb, you will want those dates blocked on HomeAway as well. One way to accomplish this is to directly link the calendar on one platform with the corresponding calendar on a different platform. However, once you start adding multiple units and multiple platforms, it becomes increasingly more complicated to manage them all.

Also, you don't know which calendar is the most recent, making things even more confusing.

Fortunately, there is a better way to link your platform calendars on multiple platforms. We use a channel manager that also hosts our direct booking website. We use the calendar on that site as the main calendar and link all the others to it. This gives us a central place to manage our availability across multiple sites and platforms and ultimately prevents a double booking.

An added side benefit to a central calendar is that you can start to automate notifications to your cleaning crew, runner, and maintenance crew based on check-ins and checkouts regardless of where the reservation originated.

SECTION EIGHT: CUSTOMER SERVICE

#73: KEEP A STACK OF GIFT CARDS OR RIDESHARE CREDITS HANDY

It's inevitable that things will go wrong. Someone will smoke illegal substances in your unit and leave a bad smell for the next guest. Someone will have a large family reunion within a unit that can only hold 8 people and disturb the neighbors. A crazy drunk woman will follow one of your guest's home from the bar and bang on the door at 3 a.m. in the morning then go bang on the neighbor's door (All of these things actually happened!!). It's going to happen. Be prepared.

When bad things happen, give gifts. When the next guest checks in after the illegal substance smokers, they will let you know what happened. A gift card can go a long way to smooth things over after you've taken care of the problem and apologized for the inconvenience.

When someone has a family reunion at your unit and takes up all the parking spaces for the permanent residents, you will hear about it. After you've apologized for the inconvenience, a nice gift card for the neighbors will let them know that you are truly sorry and that you value the community.

When a crazy drunk woman follows one of your guest's home and bangs on the neighbor's door at 3 a.m., screaming and shouting, the police will come. When the police come, give gifts.

#74: BE PERSONABLE YET PROFESSIONAL WHEN COMMUNICATING WITH GUESTS

Communication with your current and potential guests is a critical skill to learn. One of our mentors described our mission like this: "We strive to treat our guests with generosity and a friendly demeanor". Everything about your business should be customer focused. Remember always that you are providing an experience, not just a place to sleep. That experience starts and ends with your communication.

The first thing to remember is that you are likely serving guests from a variety of different backgrounds. They are different ages, come from different economic backgrounds, different cultures, and perhaps even different parts of the world. They will have different sensibilities, use different words, they may even think differently than you do. Each guest is coming for a different reason. They may be staying for leisure reasons. They may be staying with you because someone has a medical need and is visiting the local hospital. They may be staying with you because their house was flooded and they need temporary housing. Perhaps they are waiting on a closing to happen and need a place for their family to stay in between selling their old home and moving into a new one. Whatever the situation, ask yourself "what are their needs and desires?"

Regardless of how they communicate to you, if you place yourself in a mindset of humility and service, you will be ahead of the game on how to best communicate. Sometimes this takes a thick skin and perhaps even a position of giving them the benefit of the doubt.

Always try to say yes but be professional. Ask yourself two questions. "Is this in my power to provide?" and perhaps even more importantly, "Does this work within the business systems that we have created?" Always work within your systems. If you don't, you will ultimately break them.

Always use positive language when speaking to a guest. Words like "kindly", "please", and "thank you" should be in most every communication. Speak to others as you would expect to be spoken to. Especially when they are difficult! Be personable, but always stay professional.

#75: ALWAYS LEAVE REVIEWS FOR GUESTS, GOOD OR BAD

You as a host know how important it is to get positive reviews from guests. But it's also important that you leave honest feedback about your guests. This allows other hosts to know what to expect when this person stays with them. But it can get a little complicated at times. Here are some guidelines for leaving reviews for guests, good or bad.

Most booking platforms such as Airbnb and VRBO will send a reminder to you and your guest to leave a review after the stay is over. Guests will review you, your space and their overall experience. You review how the guest treated your space as far as cleanliness and following the house rules is concerned. Typically, once both you and your guests have left a review, you will be able to see the review. On Airbnb and VRBO, you both have a period of time to leave a review. If you suspect that a review will be bad, it's best to wait until the last minute. You'll likely have other stays and other reviews so the bad one will get buried because reviews are posted by stay, not when a review is submitted.

It is possible to automate your reviews, but it's important to have lots of different templates to choose from so that your review sounds more personal. Say things like "(Guest name) was a great guest! We would be happy to host you any time!". You have 500 characters to use but you don't have to use all of them. Be honest but be concise. Write about the communication that you had with your guest before, during and after their stay. You can talk about their cleanliness. Were they messier than most other guests? Did the cleaning crew have to do more cleanup, or did they remake the beds and it looked like no one even stayed there?

Some questions to consider answering in your review are:

1. Would you recommend this guest to other hosts?

2. Did the guests follow the house rules?

3. What was your communication like with this guest?

Remember that your review will be published on the guest's profile for all to see. You can also leave private feedback for them as well if there's anything personal that you would like to say to them.

#76: USE GUEST FEEDBACK TO YOUR ADVANTAGE

We love it when guests make recommendations on how we can improve. We are always looking for ways to make our guest's stays more enjoyable. That's our mindset. Nothing is going to be perfect the first time you do it. You can feel like you've thought of everything, but someone will come up with something that you had never thought of before. So be open to new ideas and suggestions from anyone, especially guests because those are the people you are trying to serve. And if one person suggests it, someone else will appreciate it, too.

We have had many suggestions from guests which

have helped us improve. Some of the tips in this book were even inspired by guest feedback! One guest coming for a wedding suggested that we put in a full-length mirror. So now it's something that we provide in all our units.

Another guest who liked to cook suggested that we supply nonstick cooking pans. Traditionally, we had been buying stainless cookware sets, but this guest said that stainless doesn't work as well as nonstick. Now, based on this suggestion, we supply nonstick cooking pans in our units. These are just a few examples of how future guests can benefit from a previous guest's suggestion.

Taking into consideration guest feedback is a powerful way to incrementally improve the service that you provide. One word of caution, not every piece of advice that you receive will be valid. It's up to you to determine if the feedback you're given is applicable to the customer type that you are serving.

SECTION NINE: SHORT-TERM RENTAL BUSINESS MINDSET

#77: INVEST IN YOUR TEAM

As a business owner, it can be challenging to put together a winning team. But that's what you're doing when you run a short-term rental business. And you need to have that business owner mindset from the beginning.

Every member of your team is their own person. They have their own strengths and weaknesses. They have different personalities. They have their own interests. It can be difficult as the business owner to get everyone on the same page, but it's imperative to your bottom line.

The first thing you need to do is to make sure that

everyone understands his/her role in the business. The cleaner cleans. The runner runs. The maintenance technician maintains. Each person needs to understand what his/her role is and how to do it the way you want it done and as efficiently as possible. Training is key here. If you don't teach them how you want it done, how will they know? If you don't provide feedback, good and bad, how will they know how good of a job they are doing?

The next thing you need to do is meet with each member regularly to discuss issues. This is important because your cleaning company may see things on a regular basis that you need to address. For example, the runner may forget to get the dirty towels from behind the bathroom door every time. The runner may notice that the cleaners never remember to stock the K cups. The maintenance technician may notice that the stair molding keeps coming off in the same place. Discussions like these will provide valuable insight to you as the business owner.

While you are discussing issues with your team

members, ask them their opinions on how they could work more efficiently. They may have some good ideas that you hadn't thought of. Do you need to provide something for the cleaners that would help them clean more thoroughly and quickly? Does your runner have an idea on how to change up how he/she would do inventory that would save you money? Asking your team members their opinions helps them feel empowered and valued. You don't have to take all their suggestions. You're the owner of the business after all, but you can listen.

#78: CONSISTENCY IS KEY

Consistency is key in the short-term rental business because no matter how many units you have, you want your guests to have the same 5-star experience at each unit every single time. Once guests have had a 5-star experience at one of your units, they are likely to book with you again expecting the same 5-star experience they got the first time. You need to provide it for them. Repeat customers are what you want.

We have a single female that books multiple units with us every summer because she knows that we have a security system in each unit to keep her safe and a fenced-in backyard for her to bring her dog.

We also have a family that stays with us regularly when they visit the National Whitewater Center. They stay in the same unit every time because of its proximity to where they want to be and because the unit is in a safe neighborhood.

Not only will consistency bring you repeat guests, it will also force you to develop routines. You will routinely install security systems or provide sofa beds. You will routinely offer a Keurig machine and K cups. You will routinely check up on your cleaners.

One other point to note as it relates to consistency: You should be building a brand. When someone stays in one of your units, and then the next time stays in a different one, they should be able to recognize your brand. Do you use the same mattresses? Do you provide the same linens? Is your communication consistent? When can they expect to receive their door codes? If there is a problem, what is your response time?

It requires consistent effort to provide a 5-star experience for each guest every time. Being consistent is the difference between success and failure in this business.

#79: BE WILLING TO SWALLOW YOUR PRIDE AND ADMIT WHEN YOU MAKE A MISTAKE. MISTAKES ARE HOW YOU LEARN.

We would all probably prefer to be perfect, but if you have operated for any time at all, you know that is not realistic. So, what do you do when you or your company makes a mistake or drops the ball? You admit to the mistake and take action to correct it.

It's going to happen. Your cleaning crew will forget to put out towels. You'll double book a unit. The door codes won't get changed in time. At some point, you will fall short. It's not the mistake that matters so much as your reaction to it. Most people will understand that mistakes happen, but others won't give you an inch. It's these latter situations is where you will be tested.

The key frame of mind to have is to realize that this is not a real estate business. Short-term rentals are a hospitality business! Yes, you might be leveraging real estate to run your business, or you might even aspire to use the cash flow from this business to purchase real estate, but the short-term rental industry is grounded in hospitality.

Realizing that you are in the hospitality business will begin to shift your focus to your guests' needs. One of the primary needs of a guest is to feel considered. They want to feel that you are considering their wants, needs and desires, and that you are CHOOSING to serve them.

So, when you mess up or fall short of guest expectations, be willing to remain humble, admit the shortcomings, and work to fix the issue. Next, put a plan in place to make the scenario less likely to happen again. It's from our mistakes that we learn to become better hosts and business owners.

SECTION TEN: BONUS SECRETS

#80: USE DIFFERENT COLORED LAUNDRY BAGS FOR EACH PROPERTY

Here's a trick we love. We knew we needed to get the dirty linens from the unit to the laundry service and back. But as we added more units to our portfolio, it became difficult to tell which bag went with which property. We needed a way to keep the inventory the same across all our units. We tried labeling the bags with the street name of the property which worked pretty well for a while. However, that system soon became cumbersome for both cleaners and laundry service.

We also tried the bookbag-type bags, but they were too expensive and too small. As we were researching bag options, we came across different colored bags. Genius! And they are large enough to hold most of the linens (we get the 30" x 40" nylon bags). Now we can easily tell which bag goes to which property. We buy 3 bags in a specific color for each property.

This also works well to determine how to allocate your linen costs among your units. When we first started, we simply took whatever the linen service charged us that week and divided the cost between all our units. This made the accounting work out overall, but if we wanted to see how one unit was doing versus another, the linen bill skewed the numbers and did not give us an accurate picture of how things really were. For example, a unit that had three checkouts in one week had more laundry to do and therefore a higher bill. Another unit that was occupied over the same period of time by only one set of guests had a much lower laundry bill. By using the different colored bags, our linen service was easily able to bill us by the color bag washed. And now we know which linen costs to allocate to each property. Another consideration along those lines is what to do if you plan on raising funds for a unit or perhaps even selling off an existing unit. Never give someone a reason to doubt your numbers!

It can seem like a pain at first, but using the different colored bags for each unit or property will not only help you control your inventory of linens, it will make your bookkeeper happy too.

#81: INVEST IN AN OZONE GENERATOR

Bad smells are inevitable. Eventually, you are going to encounter a guest that decides to smoke in the unit, or perhaps in one of your pet friendly units, a guest brings a dog that wasn't quite as house-trained as you were led to believe. Perhaps your guests are really into cooking their own seafood! In situations like this, you are going to need a quick and effective way to eliminate odors before your next guest arrives.

Sometimes just having the cleaning crew do their thing takes care of the smell. Other times, air fresheners may work, but they only mask the odor for a little while. Air purifiers clean dust pollen and other particles from the air but do not necessarily remove odors.

Ozone generator to the rescue! An ozone generator is just a machine that produces, well ozone. Ozone can penetrate carpets, furniture, wall treatments, light fixtures, air ducts, and other places where smells can hide. Ozone is what makes the air smell fresh after a thunderstorm.

The only real downside to an ozone machine is that the ozone that it produces is harmful to living things including your guests and your cleaners. So, to use it the unit must be vacated and left vacant for a small amount of time once the ozone machine has been turned off. However, it is very effective and will get rid of odors that other methods will not. They're usually not available locally and something that you have to order online. Our advice is to order early before you need it and keep one on hand. You'll be glad that you did.

#82: BUY A PORTABLE AC UNIT

If your property is in an area that requires air conditioning in the warmer months, consider your plan of action when the AC unit fails during a guest's stay. Having one or more portable AC units on standby gives you a way to respond when this inevitably happens.

Portable AC units can be purchased locally and run a few hundred dollars in most cases. They typically won't work as well as a central AC unit or even a good window unit, however they can provide some relief and are better than sitting in a hot unit. You want to use them only temporarily until the main problem can be resolved. However, the goodwill that is created between you and your guests by being prepared and having a temporary solution to the problem will go a long way towards saving what could possibly be either a bad review or, even worse, a full refund.

Don't get caught scrambling to find an HVAC repair person at night or on a holiday. Be prepared!

#83: LOCK UP YOUR EXTRA TOWELS AND SUPPLIES

We have discovered that if you leave it out, guests will use it. So, if you don't want it to be used, lock it up. Towels and toilet paper are the two best examples. We've already talked about toilet paper, so let's talk towels.

Leave out only enough towels for each guest to use during their stay. We leave out 2 bath towels, 2 hand towels and 2 washcloths per guest per stay. We provide a washer and dryer in our units so guests can wash whatever they use if they would like to. Because we use a professional laundry service to wash all our linens, giving guests unlimited towels can really make our laundry bill go sky high instead of our profits.

#84: MARKET FOR DIRECT BOOKINGS

As great as the platforms are at bringing you customers, your most profitable stays will come from direct bookings. A direct booking is when a guest makes a reservation with your company directly instead of through a third-party platform like Airbnb. When a guest books their stay through a platform such as Airbnb, a percentage of the amount that they are paying goes to the platform.

Take, for example, a guest who books through Airbnb and pays $1,000 total for their stay. You as the host get $850 and the other $150 goes to the platform in the form of fees. A large portion of those fees are to cover the costs associated with acquiring that customer. And a portion of those fees are profit for the platform.

Contrast that with a direct booking where a guest pays $1,000 total for their stay. Subtract the $30 that it costs you to process their credit card and now that same booking has netted you $970. That is an extra $120 for the exact same stay. In fact, you could actually give your guests a discount and still make more money while they are paying less, creating a win-win situation.

Obviously, we want to get more direct bookings, but how do you get them? The first people you should be marketing to for direct bookings are people who have stayed with you before. Maintain a database of contact information for each guest that stays with you. This way you can market to these people to book with you directly when returning to the area. When returning guests book with you directly, you are avoiding payment of the acquisition costs to a third-party platform for the same customer. Remember, a portion of the fees incurred are for bringing you the customer in the first place. By not paying a third party for the same customer, your profitability improves.

Where you choose to market for direct bookings next will depend heavily on who your target customer is. For example, if you are targeting families with children like we are, you might network with Real Estate Agents. Real Estate Agents often have clients who are moving to the area and looking for a new home. These clients need places to stay and many times desire to get a feel of what it's like to live in a particular area of town. Your short-term rentals may be the perfect solution for this type of customer. Agents also will have clients in situations where they are in between homes. They may have sold their existing home, but their new home isn't ready to be moved into yet. These clients, too, need temporary housing. Insurance agents and adjusters may be another source of direct booking referrals. If a person's house floods, for example, making it unlivable, they are likely to be one of the first to know. Perhaps you are serving medical professionals. The Human Resources Department at your local hospital or a staffing agency may be a place to visit. If business travelers are your bag, market your services to local corporations.

Marketing for direct bookings should be a part of every short-term rental business. There are many advantages to increasing the number of direct bookings that your business receives over time. Not only does it increase your bottom line, it helps to build your unique brand. It also reduces your reliance on third party platforms. And it ultimately allows your short-term rental business to compete on an entirely different level.

#85: USE AIRBNB AS TRAINING WHEELS BEFORE YOU MOVE TO OTHER MARKETING PLATFORMS

Airbnb revolutionized the short-term rental industry by providing a relatively secure and hassle-free way for hosts and guests to find each other. But even further than that, they provided an infrastructure for payment, establishing identities, mediation in case of disputes, rules, regulations, and guidelines.

When you first start out on your short-term rental adventure, it's likely that you will want to list on Airbnb first. They have so dominated the space, that the brand is often used as a noun. People talk of staying in an "Airbnb" sometimes even if they booked on another platform. So naturally it makes sense for you to list there.

But what you may not realize or appreciate are all the back-end systems that they have put into place for you. For example, for our first year in business we were listed on Airbnb and HomeAway/VRBO. We never had a problem getting paid or had a bad experience with either. While most of our bookings came through Airbnb, there were a significant amount that came through HomeAway as well. So, when we started adding more units after that first year, we simply did as we had always done and listed on both platforms. Our very first guest from HomeAway in one of our new units turned out to be one of our worst. It was everything that you hear about in a horror story. They trashed the house, smoked in the unit, broke glasses, damaged furniture, and more. We did what we normally do and sent the guest a payment request for the damages. At this point, the guest called their credit card company and disputed the entire stay! When we inquired with HomeAway, they asked us to provide a copy of the signed rental agreement and a copy of their photo identification. Well, we didn't have either one of those things! We believed, wrongly, that HomeAway/VRBO was the same as Airbnb. Had this been an Airbnb reservation, they would have already collected all this information and would have advocated on our behalf. We lost the entire reservation amount and had to pay for all the damages ourselves. It was a hard lesson to learn, but we now know that it's important to require a rental agreement and a photo ID for our guests that come from any platform besides Airbnb. And that's just one example.

There are many other differences that we could point out. The point is that if you don't already have the systems in place (and experience) to deal with the extra steps required for platforms outside of Airbnb, wait. Lean on the service that they provide and take the time to gain some experience and get your systems in place before venturing to other platforms. At least if something goes wrong, you'll have someone to call. Otherwise, things may be just fine... until they are not!

#86: KEEP A COPY OF ALL OF YOUR KEYS AS BACKUP

This may seem obvious, but in practice it's something that you really need to develop a system for. If you are using smart locks with key codes like we do, then you can tend to become complacent about having the actual physical keys available as a backup. Almost any smart lock will come with a physical key in case the lock isn't otherwise working. The challenge is that they all look alike, and in the haste and excitement of setting up your units, you may forget just which set of keys goes to which lock. Was that the key for the front door or the supply closet?

Batteries die and electronics malfunction. As you

install each lock, label the accompanying set of keys and store them in a secure location. When the need for the appropriate key arises, you'll be glad that you took the time to be prepared. Also, you'll get to use your label maker!

#87: LABEL YOUR SWITCHES

It's a fact that we love the label maker. It's probably really obvious when you walk into one of our units because we label EVERYTHING, even the light switches. It's really annoying when you think you're going to turn on the kitchen light, but you turn on the garbage disposal instead. Label maker to the rescue! There are so many switches in the kitchen that a guest, who has never been there before, would have no idea what switch controlled what. There's a switch for the lights. There's a switch for the garbage disposal. There's a switch for the dishwasher, and if it's not on, the dishwasher won't work. Then you get guests messaging you after they've left saying they couldn't get the dishwasher to start. Then all the dishes will be dirty when the cleaners show up and they have to wash them by hand. Solution? Label it. Label them all. Label the dishwasher with a label that says "Switch on wall must be turned on to work" or something like that. Some people say a diamond is a girl's best friend. Wynde says a label maker is a girl's best friend!

#88: DON'T WAIT UNTIL YOUR UNIT IS READY TO LIST IT

Most people seem to feel that they can't list their space on a platform like Airbnb until they have everything done and the pictures are taken. However, this is not the case. As soon as you determine your "go live" date, create the listing for your new unit. For the picture, create a generic "coming soon" picture that you can use until your unit is complete and your professional photos are ready. Block off your calendar until the date you plan to be ready for guests. That way, it won't get booked before it is complete. Next, make the listing active. You will be surprised how many people will book your listing even without pictures! Of course, you will get a lot of inquiries wondering if you have any pictures available. We tell the truth; that we are waiting on professional photos, but this unit will be comparable in quality to our existing units. Usually that is enough to secure the booking. By listing your unit early before it is ready, you can have guests arrive the very day that you are open for business! We started doing this with our second unit and have been doing it ever since with great success.

ABOUT THE AUTHORS

John and Wynde Williams are a husband and wife team that own and operate Queen City Suites, a short-term rental company based in Charlotte, NC.

You can follow their adventures on Facebook @TheCashFlowCouple or on YouTube as The Cashflow Couple.

You can also reach them via their website at www.thecashflowcouple.com

Made in the USA
Middletown, DE
17 January 2021

31810797R00144